In the pages of history, no city is more glamorous than Babylon.

Its name evokes pictures of wealth. Its treasures of gold and jewels were fabulous.

You might think forests, mines, and the sea surrounded such a wealthy city.

That was not the case.

Babylon was located beside the Euphrates River in a flat, arid valley. It had no forests, no mines—not even stone for building.

Yet, Babylon became the wealthiest city in the world due to its hard-working and well-educated inhabitants who understood the Laws of Gold.

In this majestic city lived a girl called Sarai. She didn't wear the most expensive clothes like some of her friends. She didn't have servants like some of her cousins. She didn't possess the most extravagant jewelry like some of her neighbors.

Her small, beautiful room had a balcony that overlooked the great city. Sarai would frequently observe the busy lives of the city's inhabitants. Sellers would wake up early in the morning to display their goods on the street; kids would hurry with their parents to school; water carriers would walk from the distant Euphrates river to the workers at the wall.

Yet, something always caught Sarai's attention. Atop one of the hills, she could see the villas of the wealthiest families, with a massive palace on top.

"If I could only live there," she would often say. "I would be the happiest girl in Babylon."

Her father knew about her affliction. One afternoon, as she was arriving home, her father said:

"Sarai, I want to tell you a story. I think you're old enough to learn the struggles our family has faced."

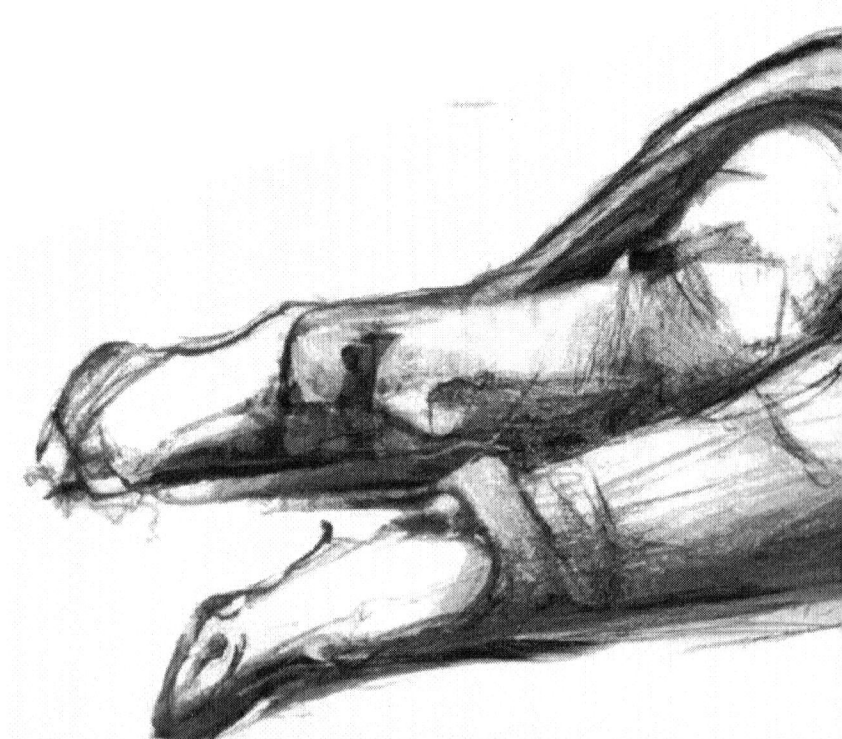

Sarai sat down across the desk from her father.

Her father continued, "Did you know that your grandfather was once homeless?"

Sarai looked attentively at her father as he continued. "His parents abandoned him when he was your age; his uncle, the only relative he had, did not even offer his sympathies. Your grandfather was utterly alone.

"He lived on the street for days, begging for food. Eventually, a man pitied him and offered him work.

"You might think that your grandfather's situation improved, but that wasn't so. Your grandfather worked as a water carrier. He would fetch water from the Euphrates River and walk through the burning sands for hours."

"Many with the same job perished, yet your grandfather found joy at the thought of providing a valuable service to those who needed it."

Sarai's eyes widened.

"I never told you this story, Sarai. I never told you how your grandfather became one of Babylon's wealthiest and most educated men.

"Your grandfather believed in hard work and discipline. He never borrowed. He treasured work above all things and would never give me a single gold coin I would use for a wrong purpose.

"Those who met your grandfather later in life say he was a greedy man, but he protected everything he had built throughout his lifetime.

"Others say that your grandfather was selfish and that he wouldn't help the poor. Listen: He donated to charity and gave scores more than

those who spoke wrongly about him.

"The water carriers he met early in life became jealous about his wealth; so they believed he obtained it illegally; through stealing.

"Your grandfather was born poor, but he became a prosperous man in wealth, intelligence, education, and virtue.

"Why didn't you tell me this story before?" Sarai asked.

Her father continued, "Sarai, money can help you enjoy the best the world has to offer. From the most delicate dresses made of silk from the Far East to hosting the most prominent feasts for your guests to traveling to Egypt, Rome, and Greece.

"The palace you see on top of those hills belonged to Arkad, once The Richest Man in Babylon.

"He held the most considerable wealth not only in Babylon but in every other city in the world. He was more prosperous than anyone before him, and some say he was more affluent than the king.

"Despite his wealth, his descendants faced incredible hardships. That palace is no longer in Arkad family's hands, as they were unprepared for the wealth that befell them.

"Some of Arkad's descendants are doing fine, but others left the city to pursue riches in Greece, while many others are in an endless legal battle over the last remains of Arkad's wealth.

"The wealth of Arkad didn't leave his heirs prosperity; it led many of them to ruin. Arkad knew how to make gold; his wisdom helped countless men become rich. But Arkad was terrible at distributing his wealth and even less adept at leaving a legacy.

"Sarai, I don't want the same fate to fall upon our family. I want us to be a supportive family that can help each other during tough times. I want you to love your brother and sister and support each other no matter what.

"Your grandfather learned the lesson well; He never spoiled me with undeserved riches as that would have meant my ruin. He only provided for my food and education. Everything else we have, I acquired myself through hard work.

"You're growing quickly. It feels like it was only yesterday when you were running around with the other kids. It won't be long until you become a young woman; you will face tough decisions soon enough.

"Sarai, you can be anything you wish.

"You can build the fastest chariots the world has ever seen.

"You can become a prosperous merchant, importing wares from China and Egypt.

"Do you remember when you helped build a clay house for those poor children? You can become an architect and provide elaborate plans for the king's numerous construction projects.

"You also have great easiness with your words; you can become a diplomat, travel to foreign lands, and form strong relations with other nations.

"Sarai, you have even shown promise as a doctor. I remember when you cured your cousin's hand. The field of medicine is expanding at an accelerating pace. You can heal people's sicknesses by learning about Greek medicine.

"No matter your choice of occupation, I will always support you, but promise me this:

"The same Sun that shines today will shine again tomorrow. But that doesn't mean that the good times will last forever.

"There will come a time, very distant or not so much, when I will not be there for you. So heed your grandfather's advice, just like I did."

Sarai's father got up and picked up a small wooden box. Seven small tablets lay inside.

"I was your age when my father handed me these seven tablets. He told me these words: 'I want to give you the secrets I learned from Arkad. These secrets led me to prosper both in wealth and virtue.'

"Sarai, I want you to have them, so you will always be prosperous when times are good or bad.

"When you face difficulties in life, go back and read them. The wisdom you seek is in them.

"These tablets, made of nothing more than wood and clay, hold the secrets that would have made many rich and would have prevented the loss of countless fortunes, even the wealth of Arkad's family."

Sarai was curious about the tablets. How could those old pieces of clay hold such secrets?

She grabbed them and read the following:

Tablet #1:

Gold comes gladly and in increasing quantity to those who save at least ten percent of all their earnings from as early an age as possible.

Tablet #2:

Gold works diligently for the wise owner who finds profitable employment, multiplying like the field flocks.

Tablet #3:

Gold holds itself to the protection of the cautious owner who invests it under the advice of those wise in its handling.

Tablet #4:

Gold slips away from those who invest it in businesses or purposes with which they are unfamiliar or not approved by wise persons.

Tablet #5:

Gold flees those who would force it to impossible earnings, follow the alluring advice of tricksters and schemers, or who trusts it to his inexperience and romantic desires in investment.

"A few years after my father gave me those tablets, he sent me to Egypt.

"All he gave me was these seven tablets and a bag of gold that should have lasted until I found an occupation.

"I was scared; I knew nobody and wasn't even sure what the inscriptions on the tablets meant.

"The road to Egypt was brutal; it was a two-month-long journey. The sands were hot, and I desired to return home to my family.

"To make matters worse, numerous thieves and bandits were on the road.

"But I remembered my father's wisdom, and I had no choice but to continue my journey.

"I was close to my destination when I stopped at the Faiyum Oasis.

"My father's sack of gold was still almost full, so I had no trouble paying for my expenses.

"Next to the oasis, I saw a group of men playing a game; they seemed to be having a lot of fun.

"They asked me if I wanted to try my luck by playing dice. If the dice fell on one number, I would multiply my money fivefold. If it didn't, I would lose it.

"I decided to risk one coin, but my losses kept piling up as I played.

"Eventually, I lost everything, including my camel. The men who had seemed so friendly walked away, leaving me with nothing. I later learned that the men rigged the dice beforehand, a popular method they used to trick trav-

elers into losing their gold.

"I had no choice but to continue on foot, and a long week passed that I still do not dare remember.

"I remember seeing a light in the desert. Sarai, I thought I was dead. As I got closer, I saw the peak of an enormous monument: The Great Pyramid of Giza.

"It was much bigger than anything I had ever seen. I couldn't believe that someone could build something so enormous.

"I reached the city of Memphis in Egypt looking awful. My thorn clothes made me look like a vagabond, and I hadn't eaten in days.

"With hard work and perseverance, I found an occupation; a camel merchant hired me. I was responsible for looking after some of his camels, ensuring they were fed appropriately.

"It was hard, grueling work. I read and re-read the seven tablets.

"As soon as I received my first pay of twenty copper coins, I saved two of them.

"Every time I made a deposit into my ever-growing treasure, I smiled. Seeing my copper coins turn into silver and ultimately into gold made me feel happiness amidst the great misery I was experiencing. Every day I became more determined to increase my savings, to the point where I saved half of my income.

"Within two years, I had saved three gold coins to buy a camel.

"As dealing with camels was something I had experience with, I could buy a camel for a reasonably good price that I later resold for four gold coins, making me six months' worth of savings in just two days.

"My treasure grew steadily and surely. As others saw me being successful and not spending money, they must have realized I had gold. The tricksters appeared surely enough, trying to offer me schemes to double my money quickly, but I had learned my lesson and decided to continue working in the business I knew.

"After I made back all the gold that I had lost; not only tripled it but multiplied it tenfold, I returned to Babylon.

"Your grandfather was by then an old man. Amid his wrinkles, I saw his happiness of seeing me."

"I was worried about you," he said.

He then handed me five handkerchiefs.

He said: "My time on this Earth is ending. Please pass on these handkerchiefs to your chil-

dren when the time is right. My son, my sight has failed me. Will you read them out loud so I can hear them again?"

Handkerchief #1: Start Your Bag of Gold to Grow

If you want your treasure to grow, you must start to save more. Aim for at least 10%, but save as much as possible.

Don't be cheap with what matters and those you love, but you'll save more by refraining from needless expenses. You will start to see your balance grow, bringing great happiness to your soul.

And remember these wise words: "Get what you can, and what you get hold—This is the secret that turns stone into gold."

Handkerchief #2: Protect Your Treasure From Loss

Always protect your treasure, for others want it more than you realize. You will face numerous obstacles in life, more than I can count. There's no end to the creativity of the tricksters who want your gold. I can tell you this: Trust in the council of wise men who care about you.

It's much better to refrain from an investment than to experience great regret.

Handkerchief #3: Increase your ability to earn.

No matter your vocation, you will find competition. "The basement is crowded," some would say, "but there's plenty of room at the top." To do well, you must increase your ability to earn. And there's no other path than through study and practice.

Do well in your studies, and you increase your chances tenfold. Start practicing what you want to become the best at, and your chances increase a hundredfold. You must focus on whatever you decide to pursue until you become the best in your craft.

Being mediocre is common; there are mediocre people in every occupation. Once you find what you're passionate about, don't look to the right or the left. Focus on your path and become the best.

Handkerchief #4: Invest in Thy Dwelling

No possession can change your life as much as a home. No family can fully enjoy life unless they have a plot of ground wherein children can play on the clean Earth and where the owner may raise blossoms and good rich herbs to feed a family.

Many blessings come to the person who owns their own home. And it will significantly reduce the cost of living, making more of their earnings available for gratifications and desires.

Handkerchief #5: Provide in Advance for Your Needs and the Needs of Your Family

There's nothing more certain in life than the fact that we grow old. The wrinkles in my face and the gray hairs on my head lay testament to this.

Now I have many friends who failed to heed this advice and wasted their money on things that were not useful and are now lamenting poverty.

As Sarai's father finished reminiscing the wisdom imparted on the five handkerchiefs, Sarai burst out crying. "Dad, I want you to always be with me."

"I know, and there's nothing that I'd like more in this world than for that to be the case, but it's not the world's Law for such a thing to exist. The cycle of life continues, and there will come a time when I, your father, who you see as a powerful man, will return to the dust. The same will happen to you, and if you choose to have children of your own, to them as well.

"Now you know the truths of the world. You know how to create, store and invest your gold. It's time for you to go out into the world and make your path.

"I will always be there for you, but I cannot give you everything you desire since I want the best for you.

"I wish I could. I do. I wish I could buy you all those fancy dresses from the Far East.

"But if I did, you'd have everything you wanted, and I know this: Misfortune befalls those who don't work for their gold.

"Go ahead, be a strong girl. Choose your career wisely, grow your earning potential, save, and invest. If you want any advice, I'm here for you.

"I want a life of luxury for you—a life where you don't have to worry about paying bills or making ends meet.

"But I want you to stand up for yourself and be a strong girl. There's no more remarkable accomplishment for me as a father than to see you succeed.

"Sarai, I love you and always will. Let us feast and remember this day when I shared my father's wisdom with you, which allowed me to become the man I am."

Sarai got up, crying. She understood the wise words of her father. As she hugged him, he spoke thus:

"There's one more thing I want you to know.

"This is a warning of sorts.

"There are many dangers you will face in this world.

"And there's one that worries me the most.

"It's the allure of easy money and no more.

"In your life, you will be tempted to gamble. You will be tempted to invest your treasure furiously. You will be tempted to partake in degenerate endeavors unworthy of you. You will be tempted to accept riches from strangers who do not deserve you.

"Some of them will be offered directly, but others are much more insidious.

"It is the way of the world. The person who seeks easy riches will find misfortune, if at all.

"There are no easy riches in the world, and nobody will give you anything for free, except for your family, that loves you more than you can imagine.

"Heed these words; heed them well.

"I want you to do better than me. I want you to suppress me in every way. And I'm sure in time you will.

"So you must not stumble upon these rocks, for they are far too numerous and come in many forms.

"My beloved daughter, I want you to become the wealthiest girl in Babylon: Not in wealth, but in intelligence, education, and virtue. Those qualities are more important than all the gold in the king's coffers.

"Come on now, my girl, let us feast. But promise me this. Promise me you'll never forget. You'll read the five clay tablets and look at the handkerchiefs, knowing fully that your future rests on them. And more importantly, promise this: You'll never seek or accept easy money in any way, for the devil is always behind it."

Sarai hugged her father, and a tear rolled down her other eye. She understood.

And then she realized something more profound: She already had everything she wanted.

She had the most loving family in Babylon, the knowledge to succeed in her endeavors, and great virtue. She was already the Richest Girl in Babylon.

Manufactured by Amazon.ca
Bolton, ON